DATE DUE

AP 09 01			

$14.00   #62028

The Library of Intergenerational Learning

Native Americans™

Crow Children and Elders Talk Together

E. Barrie Kavasch

The Rosen Publishing Group's
PowerKids Press™
New York

To the Crow People, with respect for their amazing history and bright future

Published in 1999 by The Rosen Publishing Group, Inc.
29 East 21st Street, New York, NY 10010

Copyright © 1999 by The Rosen Publishing Group, Inc.

First Edition

Book Design: Danielle Primiceri

Photo Credits: Cover and all inside photos by A.J. Group, John Bacolo.

Kavasch, E. Barrie.
     Crow children and elders talk together/by E. Barrie Kavasch.
          p.   cm.—(Library of intergenerational learning. Native Americans)
     Summary: Explores the culture and traditions of the Crow Indians through the voices of a young girl, her father, and several other older people.
     ISBN 0-8239-5231-2
     1. Crow Indians—Juvenile literature. 2. Indians of North America—Great Plains—Juvenile literature.   [1. Crow Indians. 2. Indians of North America—Montana.] I. Title. II. Series: Kavasch, E. Barrie. Library of intergenerational learning. Native Americans.
     E99.C92K38   1998
     978'.0049752—dc21   98-22050
                                                                                                                       CIP
                                                                                                                        AC

Manufactured in the United States of America

Contents

I Am Crow

"My name is Carina Deputee. I am five years old and I am proud to be Crow Indian. My family and I live in St. Xavier, Montana. I go to kindergarten at the Lodge Grass School where my dad works. My mom and dad are very special to me.

"I love my great-grandma Edna Dust. She is a very **traditional** (truh-DIH-shuh-nul) lady. My favorite color is pink. I like to put it in my coloring books. My favorite game is Duck-Duck-Goose. We play this game at school."

The Crow are **descendants** (de-SEND-ents) of the Great Plains Indians of the past, who rode their horses across the rough land. Their **ancestors** (AN-ses-terz) have lived on this land for hundreds of years. The Crow **reservation** (reh-zer-VAY-shun) is in southern Montana. More than 9,300 Crow Indians live there today.

One of Carina's favorite things to do is draw and color beautiful pictures. ▶

Elders

"Carina and I enjoy visiting with everyone at the Crow Fair Campgrounds. This is where our family stays during big **celebrations** (seh-leh-BRAY-shunz)," says Ken Deputee. "My wife, Justine, and I have raised four boys and one girl. Now that they are grown, we love spending time with Carina. We are proud of our Crow traditions, and we teach them to Carina.

"This is my first year as principal of the Lodge Grass School in Lodge Grass, Montana," says Ken. "Before becoming the principal, I was a teacher for sixteen years. I worked hard to get where I am today."

Crow elders like Ken are respected for their **knowledge** (NAH-lij). They teach the younger **generations** (jeh-ner-AY-shunz) about Crow history and the ways of the world.

◀ *Carina enjoys learning about her Crow history from her father, Ken Deputee.*

Clans

"Our **clan system** (KLAN SIS-tem) is strong. It is one of four major Crow **customs** (KUS-tumz) that we **honor** (ON-er)," says Ken Deputee. "I am Piegan Clan, which follows my mom's clan. I am also a child of my father's Ties in the Bundle Clan. Clan members look after each other and help each other grow by doing the right things. Some of our other clans are the Bad War Deeds, Whistling Water, Greasy Mouth, and Big Lodge."

Crow customs also honor the sweat lodge **rites** (RYTS) and prayers, the pipe **ceremony** (SEHR-eh-moh-nee), and the **sacred** (SAY-kred) Tobacco Society. Tobacco is a sacred plant for the Crow. It **symbolizes** (SIM-bul-eye-zez) the birth of all plants and animals each spring.

The Crow may have adopted some modern things from the world around them. But their history will always be a part of their lives. ▶

Christian **missionaries** (MIH-shuh-nayr-eez) came to live among the Crow Indians in the early 1880s. They started St. Xavier mission on the banks of the Bighorn River. Some Crow became Christian. But most Crow keep their traditional religion and beliefs. The clan system is strong.

Celebrations

"Our biggest celebration is the Crow Fair Rodeo and Powwow," says Carina. "It's held each year in August. One area along the Little Bighorn River becomes the 'Teepee Capital of the World.' There are so many teepees! All of our friends and relatives bring their teepees. It is an exciting time to visit and tell stories. My dad tells very good stories!"

The Crow people celebrate many things in life. God, nature, and the spirits of their ancestors are honored in every celebration. Many people wear their most special clothes, especially the drummers and dancers, during these celebrations. Special symbols on their clothes can tell you what family, clan, or society they belong to.

◀ *The special clothes worn during Crow celebrations are often decorated with beads, feathers, and ribbons.*

An Elder's Story

It is always a special time when an elder tells the Crow Creation Story. Long ago, in the earliest times, Old Man Coyote was lonely. So with the help of two wild ducks he began to create the earth, other animals, and people. There were many adventures as Old Man Coyote created all things on the earth.

The Creation Story is a very long story, so it cannot be told here. But Crow elders still tell this story to their children. This story tells us that animals, plants, people, and natural forces are all equal and share some of the same feelings.

An elder's story can teach you about parts of your history that you may not have known about. ▶

The Land

"*Kahay*, or welcome to the land of the *Apsaalooka*, the Children of the Large-Beaked Bird. This land is sacred to us," says Clara White Hip Nomee. Clara White Hip Nomee holds two important positions. She is a respected Crow elder. She is also the madame chairperson of the Crow Tribal Council in Crow Agency, Montana. "We consider the earth our Mother. We are told by the elders that all Crow are blessed with three mothers: the earth, our natural mother, and our teepees or lodges.

"We have more than 2 million acres of land. We used to have more land, but much of it has been taken by the United States government. No matter how much land is taken from us, these ancient lands are always filled with special meaning."

Crow land is beautiful, and the Crow people respect and take care of it. ▶

"My name is Dorothy Aragon. I am Whistling Water Clan. The elders in my life are very important to me. My mother is 90 years old. I visit her every weekend. She is full of knowledge. I am always learning new things from her.

"I have ten children. I am proud of my 24 grandchildren, and now I have nine great-grandchildren. Our Crow traditions tell us we are all one big family. We all raise the grandchildren and great-grandchildren.

"I work with students at the Wyola Elementary School in Wyola, Montana. I studied hard to get to where I am today. My daughter Theresa works with our Head Start Program. I like to watch the generations grow in this program and everywhere on the reservation."

◀ *The Aragon family members support and help each other.*

Ceremonies

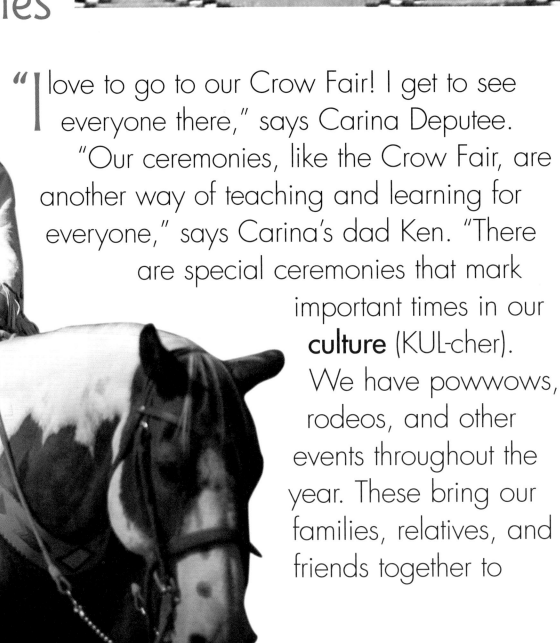

"I love to go to our Crow Fair! I get to see everyone there," says Carina Deputee. "Our ceremonies, like the Crow Fair, are another way of teaching and learning for everyone," says Carina's dad Ken. "There are special ceremonies that mark important times in our **culture** (KUL-cher). We have powwows, rodeos, and other events throughout the year. These bring our families, relatives, and friends together to celebrate and visit, share food, and tell stories. Crow children are the pride and future of our culture. They are celebrated in many ways in Crow ceremonies."

Perhaps the most important ceremony each year is the Sun Dance, which celebrates **renewal** (re-NOO-ul). It is a very important religious ceremony that is usually held in late summer. Only members of the Crow tribe can go to this ceremony.

Crow ceremonies are a big part of Crow culture. Everyone takes part in these traditional events.

Prayers and Respect

"Our religious life is an important part of our lives," says Clara White Hip Nomee. Both religion and prayer are a big part of Crow life. Crow prayers always remember the children and elders. Every family is honored in ceremonial prayers.

These prayers are special. The powerful sounds of Crow dance songs join the beating of drums. Crow dances, songs, and drums blend together as prayers are said to the Creator.

◀ *The elders believe that the Creator likes to see the Crow people celebrate and pray.*

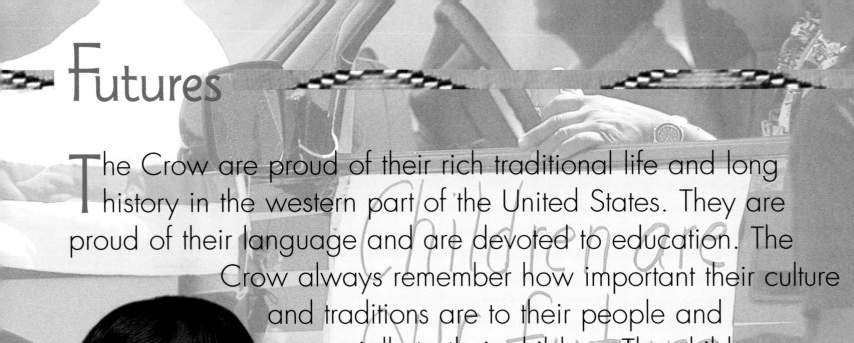

Futures

The Crow are proud of their rich traditional life and long history in the western part of the United States. They are proud of their language and are devoted to education. The Crow always remember how important their culture and traditions are to their people and especially to their children. The children are always learning about their culture and history from their elders and parents.

"We are all students and we are all teachers," says Ken Deputee. "Our last great chief, Chief Plenty Coup, believed in education. We remember our great chief's words and our history as we look toward our bright future."

Glossary

ancestor (AN-ses-ter) A relative who lived long before you.

celebration (seh-leh-BRAY-shun) Enjoying a special time in honor of something.

ceremony (SEHR-eh-moh-nee) A special activity done at certain times.

clan system (KLAN SIS-tem) A group of people who are related within a tribe.

culture (KUL-cher) The beliefs, customs, art, and religions of a group of people.

custom (KUS-tum) The accepted, respected way of doing something that is passed down.

descendant (de-SEND-ent) A person born of a certain group of people.

generation (jeh-ner-AY-shun) People born in the same twenty-year time period.

honor (ON-er) To show admiration and respect for someone or something.

knowledge (NAH-lij) Knowing something.

missionary (MIH-shuh-nayr-ee) A person who teaches a religion to the people of another country.

renewal (re-NOO-ul) Making new or pure again.

reservation (reh-zer-VAY-shun) An area of land set aside by the government for American Indians to live on; called reserve in Canada.

rite (RYT) A serious ceremony.

sacred (SAY-kred) Something that is highly respected and considered very important.

symbol (SIM-bul) A design that stands for something else.

tradition (truh-DIH-shun) To do things the way that a group of people has done them for a long time.

Index